DUTCH LANDSCAPES

BUDAPEST MUSEUM
OF FINE ARTS

DUTCH LANDSCAPES

by Ágnes Czobor

TAPLINGER PUBLISHING COMPANY
NEW YORK

Translated by
EDNA LÉNÁRT

Jacket, cover and typography by
LAJOS LENGYEL

Whether the artist picks as his subject the face of his beloved, his boots, or a piece of antiquity, it is all the same as far as art is concerned. That is what Goethe declared, he, true child of his time; his artistic taste and his activity as an art collector bear out this statement. Apart from the plaster-casts made after antique statues he bought drawings and engravings of 17th-century Dutch masters who used to draw every feature of their family members, their beloved, their customers, and even pieces of their garment and furniture with the same minute care as—if by any chance—they copied the Italian ruins of the antique.

The admiration for classical antiquity and the collection of 17th-century Dutch art was a characteristic duality of Goethe's age. Beside the huge head of Juno in his collection we find an etching by Jacob van Ruisdael whom he called a philosopher and poet, and we know that he was a true admirer of Rembrandt's art. Whenever Goethe was drawing—and that he often did with great pleasure—he never copied antique statues, but drew landscapes almost exclusively, several of which reminds one of Hercules Seghers' coloured etchings akin to Rembrandt's style. As is known, Goethe encouraged his painter friends to paint and draw landscapes, although in his works on art—as most aestheticians of the 18th and 19th centuries—he referred to landscape painting as an "inferior genre."

Goethe's contemporary, Prince Miklós Esterházy, the famous art collector, adapting himself to the dual taste of his age, bought for his picture gallery not only masterpieces of the Italian Renaissance and 17th-century Spanish masters, but also 17th-century Dutch paintings, in great numbers. The best part of the rich Dutch material in the Budapest Museum of Fine Arts consists of these paintings bought by Miklós Esterházy, many landscapes among them. Later—even during the past decades—the museum acquired quite a number of Dutch paintings, which prevailed also in the private collections in Hungary. In this volume we present thirty-seven pieces of one particular genre of this collection: the landscapes. Since many of the greatest and most characteristic Dutch landscape painters happen to be represented in it, we consider it proper to give, as a preliminary, a survey of Dutch landscape painting as a whole.

M. J. Friedländer's definition—"*Die Landschaft ist der Teil eines unfassbaren Ganzen*"*—is a most appropriate remark about 17th-century Dutch landscape painting. No landscape of the past centuries has so much been a "detail" of reality as were the 17th-century Dutch landscapes. What is more, nearly all genres of Dutch painting in that period are details of a whole of a world the human eye is incapable of perceiving.

Huizinga mentions the Dutch people's love for the simple, the everyday and the habitual as one of their most characteristic features. This was what inspired the Dutch painter when he grasped a scene of everyday life, the home of a burgher or a peasant, a portrait or still life, or when he painted a scenery of his homeland, a part the eye was capable to embrace—often just one or two tree-trunks in the wood —but he did it with love and devotion.

The Dutch people, or rather the Dutch burgher, has another most revealing quality: they like people to get an inside view of their most intimate life. Even today he does not curtain off his windows, does not mind if passers-by peer in and watch the family in their everyday doings. He even likes to put his life in the window. The word "window" should be accepted in the literal sense of the word. If he buys some new object he puts it in the window, for instance a new bowl with flowers changed or rearranged every day. (This activity is as common and natural for a Dutch housewife as keeping her house clean. This explains why just in the Netherlands the representation of a flower still life has become so widespread.) The Dutchman wishes to show his native land just as much as his home, his pictures and flowers. Some Dutch painters depict evocative details of lovely Dutch towns, the sea with its sandy beach and scarce vegetation, the dunes which play such an important part in Dutch life; others represent marshy lowlands with grazing cows, green meadows and woods fresh from constant humidity—but they never fail to complete their picture with a human figure, or at least a man-built house, boat or fence, to bring it into human proximity.

* Landscape represents one part of an unperceivable whole.

6

As a result of this choice of subjects the museum-goer may become familiar with the Dutch scenery, by no means abounding in bewildering natural beauties: its sea, woods, grassy land interwoven by small canals and lost in the wide horizon, rivers, meadows, tiny villages adorned with Gothic spires, towns with houses of red brick and white window-frames, and the constantly changing clouds of its sky, are depicted in greater detail than are the more fascinating French or Italian sceneries presented by the painters of these countries. Some antique ruins that were still extant in 17th-century Italy, parts of the Forum Romanum, carved stones, all lost since, may better be recognized on landscapes of Dutch painters who had travelled over Italy than on pictures of contemporary Italian masters.

In the 17th century the Netherlands were the only country in which landscape painting had developed in the form in which this term is used in the 19th century, when the painter represented a detail of an actual place.

The motif-painting of Jan van Goyen's master, Esaias van de Velde, is therefore referred to as landscape-portrait painting by L. Burchard; Huizinga, on the other hand, said Dutch landscape painting to be the opposite of Claude Lorrain's, and he was right as far as he had the art of the great local landscapists of the Netherlands (Esaias van de Velde, Jan van Goyen, Hercules Seghers, Rembrandt, Salomon van Ruysdael, Jacob van Ruisdael, Meindert Hobbema, Pieter Molyn, Aelbert Cuyp, Aert van der Neer and the countless minor masters) in mind. These masters who were active in their homeland tried to immortalize the modest details of their country with enthusiasm and devotion. A crooked tree-trunk or a row of slim poplars, a cow standing in water gently rippled by a breeze, a pink-roofed cottage standing lonely in yellow dunes under heavy rolling rainclouds, a trawler fabricated out of rough planks, or a solitary horseman in a scenery with a low horizon were looked upon as subjects worthy of their highly artistic brush.

Seventeenth-century Italian and French landscape painting is of a different character; it represents ideal landscapes which, though composed of real natural and architectural elements, are non-existent

7

in nature. This trend, often referred to as heroic landscape painting, in keeping with classical ideals, was initiated in the 16th century by Annibale Carracci inspired by Titian's background sceneries, and continued later by Domenichino, Agostino Tassi (Claude Lorrain's master) and Pietro da Cortona, to mention but the greatest. It reached its perfection with the reasoning Poussin and the dreaming Claude Lorrain. For his art, a wonderful mixture of dream-elements and reality, Claude Lorrain, the master of this genre, however, did not rely only on Italian traditions and on the classicizing reminiscences of his own country he had abandoned to escape from the rigid academic attitude. He was strongly inspired by the artistic conception of painters from the Netherlands working in Rome about 1600—the late Mannerists who created their strangely attractive, often romantic landscape painting from the traditions of Italian and Flemish painting (Jan Brueghel, Paul Bril, Roelandt Savery, etc.). In addition, Claude Lorrain was strongly influenced by an excellent German painter who died young, Adam Elsheimer. His genuine art inspired many of the above-mentioned painters from the Netherlands and was powerful enough to make an impact on two such different geniuses as Claude Lorrain and Rembrandt. Some of Elsheimer's arcadic twilight landscapes interspersed with tiny figures look almost as works by Claude Lorrain, though in smaller dimensions.

Elsheimer's approach reached the Netherlands through his pupils from Utrecht, Haarlem and Amsterdam (one of his direct followers was Pieter Lastman, Rembrandt's master), and enriched also the typically Dutch landscapists. Thus landscape painting, in contrast to the characterization by Huizinga, is not exempt from a certain influence of Claude Lorrain's precursors. Claude Lorrain himself, however, who stayed in Rome until his death (1682), was of a decisive influence on his contemporaries there, including Dutch painters, who came to be called Italianizers (Cornelis van Poelenburgh, Jan Asselyn, Claesz. Berchem, Bartolomeus Breenbergh, Jan Both, Jan Baptist Weenix, etc.), for, after returning home, they would paint Italian motives and landscape reminiscences, and their work may no longer be regarded as a counterpole of Claude Lorrain's art.

Landscape painters of such different conceptions are fairly well represented in the Dutch collection of the Budapest Museum of Fine Arts, although the number of the works is, naturally, not proportionate to the significance of the masters; some painters or schools are represented by one or two weaker pieces, others, however, by numerous excellent works (e.g. nine pictures by Salomon van Ruysdael, seven by Jan van Goyen, seven by Aert van der Neer).

Though, to our greatest regret, we do not possess any picture by two excellent early landscape painters as Esaias van de Velde and Willem Buyteweck, we are still glad to present a lovely picture of skaters by Hendrick Avercamp (Plate 1) giving us some idea also of the above two masters' art. Avercamp's winter scenery with its subtly drawn interpretation and rich colours is akin to the works of the late Mannerists at the turn of the century, but is, at the same time, a forerunner of the winter landscapes of Jan van Goyen, Aert van der Neer, Aelbert Cuyp and Jan van de Capelle. The animated scenes and elaborate details reminding of miniatures—a characteristic feature of early Dutch landscapes— proves a distinct knowledge of the works of Jan I Brueghel and his followers.

An outstanding piece of idyllic landscape painting recalling Claude Lorrain is a small picture by Dirck Dalens, a pupil of Moses van Uyttenbroeck who stood close to Elsheimer (Plates 2 and 3); it is one of the finest Dutch landscapes in Hungary. By painting tiny red harebells in a scenery of silvery-green tones the master more or less proved to be one of Corot's forerunner. The picture in this book strongly reminds one of Uyttenbroeck's or rather Claude Lorrain's works; one might almost say that he combines his greens and sky-blues in Claude Lorrain's spirit.

Cornelis van Poelenburgh is considered to be one of Claude's forerunners. He worked in Rome and Florence until 1627. His portrait of the children of Frederick V, Elector of the Palatinate (Plate 4), was painted one year after his returning home. As a genuine landscape painter in his rare portraits he put his models against an outdoor background. In his pictures of mythological or religious themes human figures play an even more subordinate role.

The paintings of Jan Asselyn, Pieter van Laer, Jan Both and Jan Baptist Weenix take the observer to a real Italian world, sometimes a very everyday one. The works of these masters may indeed said to be "Italianizing," since their art was influenced by the views of Claude Lorrain and his group. In Jan Asselyn's picture *Italian Landscape* (Plate 5) the church of SS. Giovanni e Paolo in Rome rises on the left, the banks of the Tiber, much farther in reality, can be seen to the right with some hills in the background. A characteristic feature of Dutch painters active in Italy—like Claude Lorrain's— was to combine real and imaginary details of scenery and architecture, topographically not belonging together. The surprising lifelikeness of the pieces of architecture or ruins, however, makes one assume that sketches must have been made on the spot—even though real and imaginary elements were mixing in the picture. It is known, however, that some of these painters made drawings of buildings or ruins that rigidly keep to topographic reality.

Pieter van Laer—who spent sixteen years of his life in Rome and, on account of his deformed figure, was called Bamboccio by the Italians and the group of Dutch painters known under the name of "Bent"—dealt with themes of Italian everyday life. He started a new trend, representing the life of the people, that history of art came to call *bambocciata*, and whose partisans are called *bamboccianti* to this day. Pieter van Laer was strongly influenced by the Italian Domenico Fetti who in his famous series of parables and other works often depicted simple people and everyday themes himself. In his Budapest picture entitled *Landscape With Morra-Players* (Plate 6) van Laer represents simple people, poor men trying to kill time with this fashionable game.

The Utrecht painters Jan Both and Jan Baptist Weenix were younger and belonged to the generation of the middle of the century. Jan Both was also a characteristic Italianizer who liked a landscape at sunrise or in twilight where golden sunrays take leave of a wood, some typically Italian small town or ruins. Ruins again may be seen on his picture in Budapest, *Antique Ruins on the Seashore* (Plate 7), where, in his own fashion and under Claude Lorrain's influence, the southern scenery is veiled in the misty golden light of a sunset.

Jan Baptist Weenix, like Asselyn, made a composition of a scenery and a building that did not belong together (Plates 8 and 9). The Tempio di Vespasiano is standing on the Forum Romanum in the heart of Rome, which is far from the seaport with its ornate ships and colourful bustling figures, here painted next to the temple.

The local Dutch landscape painters who always worked in their homeland, are represented by far more works in the Budapest museum than are the Italianate painters; with as many indeed that this volume can give but a very small assortment of them.

The dynamism and colourfulness of local Dutch landscapes characteristic of Jan van Goyen's early works underwent a fundamental change about 1628—30. Dynamism was replaced by tranquillity, colourfulness by monotony (kept in a single tone). The diagonally constructed composition mostly emphasized one principal element. Three masters, Esaias van de Velde, Pieter Molyn and Jan van Goyen, adapted the new attitude almost at the same time and quite independently from one another. Since the first master is not represented in the Budapest collection and the second only by a single unimportant painting, chosen for presentation have been three of van Goyen's pictures. Before discussing these, however, mention should be made of the art of Hercules Seghers who had painted in one tonality even earlier than the three above-mentioned masters. The catalogue of the Museum of Fine Arts does not keep any of Seghers' paintings in evidence, but one can get a clear idea of his art observing the background scenery of the *Parable of the Man Hiding Treasure*, attributed to Rembrandt (Plates 10 and 11). On this detail—whether really painted by Rembrandt as we believe, or by Seghers as certain scholars assume—one can recover all the features characteristic of Seghers' paintings. Under the thin and transparent layer of paint put on with infinite subtlety one can discover a brown undercoat; the tone is greyish-green, the light yellowish, the shades are brown, and the strangely crippled trees—as it is so often also with Seghers—seem to be slim haystacks. There are no figures in the background. Seghers influenced the spirit and attitude of Rembrandt, Rembrandt's followers and numerous other Dutch masters. Seghers' impact may be felt especially on Rembrandt's early landscapes, which bear the same features as his figural paintings. In his figural paintings Rembrandt emphasizes the elements of composition he considers important, strongly illuminating them, while the less important ones remain in the shade—and he does the same in his landscapes. He viewed the scenery from very far, as did Hercules Seghers; his landscapes often look as if painted from a bird's-eye view. Though he always depicted reality, still—as all strokes of his brush were directed by some psychological motive—realism on his landscapes as on his portraits or figural compositions turned to be a vision evoking an individual mood and atmosphere full of dramatic conflicts.

In the second half of the 17th century Jan van Goyen became the leading figure of Dutch landscape painting. We know a huge number of dated paintings and even more drawings by him of which only a few are meant to be sketches to his pictures. The tonality of his landscapes with low horizons, airiness offering a wide view and painted with an almost impressionistic freshness, is yellow and later bluish-grey. In his last years—like in his earliest pictures—he became more colourful again and his landscapes are veiled in the solemn tranquillity of an opening world. Van Goyen was one of the best masters of air-perspective, which was of immense importance in Dutch landscape painting. The air in the Netherlands is always hazy from frequent rain and this circumstance exerts a permanent influence on the values of tones. Few were the painters (particularly in the 17th century) who were capable of rendering this constant change of "valeurs" as excellently as Jan van Goyen (Plates 12–15).

From among his numerous followers we present a work by Wouter Knijff akin to van Goyen's œuvre in motif (Plate 16), where the admirable ease of the great master can be seen to have turned into a somewhat forced Mannerism.

The paintings of Salomon van Ruysdael can almost be mistaken for van Goyen's late pictures with their colourful tones and wide horizons. In his early pictures Ruysdael continued van Goyen's art. Though they were rather different in character—van Goyen a restless, wandering Bohemian, Ruysdael a quiet petty bourgeois—their art had much in common. In the course of his life van Goyen several times changed his way of looking at things and his style fundamentally and was interested in a great variety of motifs. Ruysdael nearly always painted the same things: a tavern among tall trees (Plates 18 and 19) with carts in front, a highway with oxen, carts or horsemen (Plate 17), a broad river with people fishing in crowded boats. At first his backgrounds were closed down like on a stage, later the horizon widened, as in van Goyen's picture, to show buildings on riverbanks and small towns in the distance. In both van Goyen's and Salomon Ruysdael's pictures the tonality prevailed over local colours. In his early period it was yellowish, then grey or vivid green, in his late pictures—like in van Goyen's—it turned to be dark grey, nearly black. The general effect, however, is not colourless, the scenery is richly peopled with staffage figures in gaudy clothes whose artistic elaboration is so subtle that they almost render an effect of 18th-century *macchiette* of Italian *vedute*. Ruysdael liked to paint trees much more than van Goyen did (who put a bare or scarcely foliated tree in the foreground just symbolically). The fact that Salomon van Ruysdael was attracted by woods and trees is attributed mostly to the influence of his more gifted nephew, Jacob van Ruisdael.

Van Goyen's influence can be felt on the works of Anthony Jansz. van der Croos who worked in The Hague; the Budapest museum treasures one of his interesting paintings (Plate 22). The bare tree in the left foreground, the hazy greyish tone and the light impressionistic rendering prove the thorough study of van Goyen's pictures.

Salomon van Ruysdael, on the other hand, was the master of Cornelis Gerritsz. Decker. His lovely, almost romantic picture with its fairy-tale atmosphere is shown here (Plate 28).

Fromentin who seriously undervalued landscape painting "for its own sake" declared Jacob van Ruisdael to be the greatest master of the Dutch school after Rembrandt. He characterized him in the following words: "*De tous les peintres hollandais, Ruisdael est celui qui ressemble le plus noblement à son pays. Il en a l'ampleur, la tristesse, la placidité un peu morne, le charme monotone et tranquille.*"*

*Of all the Dutch painters Ruisdael is the one who represents his country in the noblest manner. His art reflects its amplitude, its sadness, its somewhat sombre placidity, and its monotonous and tranquil charm.

Jacob van Ruisdael was one of the greatest landscape painters not only of his own country but of the whole 17th-century painting. He, like his uncle, came from Haarlem but worked in Amsterdam from 1656. His art, now melancholic, now romantic and often very dramatic, is characterized by a reserved attitude, sensitiveness and an emotional approach to nature. He managed to imbue even his landscapes with his poetic individuality struggling with conflicts. There is an infinite variety in his motifs: terraced scenery bathed in light with the view of a distant town in the background; the depth of a forest with old trees, the greyish streaked and knotty trunks reflected in small puddles; storm above the wood, or often repeated themes as crowds of people on a seashore, lonely romantic ruins of a castle on the edge of a forest or a pond, sometimes part of a town, the Hofvyver in The Hague, the Dam Square in Amsterdam or one of Amsterdam's other lovely districts. Even his *vedute* bear the features of a landscape. They are not rigid topographical settings but dynamic sceneries with their special atmosphere where also certain buildings are represented (Plates 24 and 25). Jacob van Ruisdael painted foreign landscapes only towards the end of his life. The craze of the wealthy bourgeoisie for foreign countries prompted him to paint Scandinavian scenery, as did Everdingen, or Swiss landscapes like those of Roghman, although he never visited any of these countries. His romantic nature shines through the high mountains, dashing cascades and pinewoods on these paintings which surpass those of Everdingen but, as his experience of foreign countries came of secondary sources, these paintings are less spontaneous and less fascinating than those made of his native land.

Jacob van Ruisdael's friend and pupil Meindert Hobbema was a less romantic but a more sober and much more intimate painter. No abandoned ruins of castles frighten the observer, but small inhabited houses and watermills engage his attention. However simple and everyday subjects Ruisdael chose for his canvases, they always have a solemn effect and make us feel nature's own wild grandeur. Hobbema, on the other hand, shows the everyday character of nature and, even though his pictures are less crowded, they convincingly prove that its landscapes are created by man. He never was as poetic as his master, but could always create atmosphere. He did not penetrate in the depth of the forest, but rather depicted the skirts where nature had been tamed for human use. His picture in the Budapest Museum of Fine Arts representing a cottage at the skirts of the forest (Plate 26) is not without traces of Ruisdael's influence.

Another follower of Jacob van Ruisdael was Vermeer II van Haarlem whose later works showed signs of the influence by Philips Koninck, a pupil of Rembrandt. Our museum has one of his fine pictures with strong Ruisdaelian character (Plate 27), showing the dunes of Overveen with the view of Haarlem. Jacob van Ruisdael himself had depicted this theme several times. Ruisdael's paintings are sunnier, airier, more colourful and dynamic than Jan Vermeer's works with their somewhat gloomy atmosphere.

The fine picture of the castle of Kostverloren (Plate 29), with its master still problematic, has much in common with the art of Hobbema, mentioned earlier, and that of another outstanding master, Jan van Kessel.

Roelof Jansz. de Vries from Haarlem painted his landscapes in Jacob van Ruisdael's style. We can observe Salomon van Ruysdael's influence on his pictures: *The Highway* and *Riverbank* (Plates 30 and 31).

We complete the circle of Jacob van Ruisdael's pupils with pictures by Jan de Lagoor (Plate 32), Simon de Vlieger (Plate 33), Jan Wynants (Plates 34 and 35) and Allaert van Everdingen (Plate 36).

Aelbert Cuyp's picture *Cows in the Water* (Plates 37 and 38) is one of the finest pieces of the Budapest museum's Dutch collection, and also one of the master's most attractive works. Though having been active in several genres, Cuyp was at his best in his landscapes. Even in the 18th century, when he was called the Dutch Claude Lorrain—and was one of the most popular painters—his airy pictures in golden hue were valued most. He painted animals with special devotion, almost with the lifelikeness of a portrait, the figures, however, had much of a summed up simplicity—almost like a 17th-century Hubert Robert. Most of his landscapes represent the neighbourhood of Dordrecht, his native town and the estuary of the Maas. Neither forests nor mountains attracted him, not even towns; what he was interested in was flatland, shallow waters with animals standing in vegetative tranquillity. This calmness is sometimes disturbed by the noise of hunters whose red coats and broad-rimmed hats lend special loveliness to his pictures.

We feel the same stillness in the work of Anthonie van Borssom from Amsterdam, *Riverbank with a Solitary Horseman* (Plate 39).

Paulus Potter was not as many-sided as Cuyp, and became generally known as the painter of animals. One could say that he was the very landscape painter to paint one "detail" of nature. His pictures are almost cuttings without any composition, they are but recording of themes inspired by nature. Thus he gives the impression of incredible modernity. He was not a dreamer, he was a naive and correct observer of nature, first and foremost of animals. Trees, scenery, grass of a vivid green are frames to his representations rather than their scenes. His early works were completely different from the later ones; they prove him to be one of the pre-Rembrandt painters and a pupil to his father, Pieter Potter. Such an early work is his fascinating picture of a shepherd and shepherdess (Plates 40 and 41), the significance of which lies in the fact that it is so much different from his accustomed and so often repeated themes.

Philips Wouwerman, too, painted animals—mainly horses and horsemen in landscapes—but his conception was quite different. Though according to our knowledge he had never been to Italy, still some Italianizing features show in his work as a result of the influence of Dutch Italianizers. His repeatedly appearing motif is a scenery with bustling life. We could best characterize his landscapes by calling them genre pictures fancifully composed in an out-of-doors scenery. His choice of subjects is most varied, what they have in common is that almost all of them are put in landscapes. He had the great gift of effortless creation which is reflected in his manner of painting.

Though he lived in Haarlem until his death he could not escape the Italianizing influence of Pieter van Laer who had settled there after his Italian tour. This may be observed on one of the finest paintings in the Budapest Museum of Fine Arts, *Rocky Landscape with Travellers at Rest*, a scenery bathed in the light of the rising sun (Plate 42).

Older than the former ones, Aert van der Neer arrived later at the maturity of his art. On one or another of his pictures, elaborated often in a graphic manner, we see a surprising freshness and naturalness. He had a refined way of discerning the atmospheric subtleties of the scenery, preferred the light of early mornings, dusk and mostly moonlit nights. He sometimes painted landscapes in complete darkness with trees of small leaves against an almost black sky. His flat, wooded, inhabited landscapes are animated with a few small figures (Plates 43 and 44).

It is not by mere chance that the characteristic genre of seascapes developed in the Netherlands (though we must not forget the Flemish masters as they strongly influenced both this and other genres); there is hardly any country where the sea is of such an importance.

Ships dominate on Simon de Vlieger's seascapes painted with strong highlights; the painting shown here is also more of a representation of ships (Plate 45).

His pupil, Willem van de Velde the Younger, who spent the last decades of his life in Britain, was the best painter of ships and sea battles. On one of his attractive early works (Plate 46) he still recalls his master's style.

A landscape by Abraham van Beyeren, a painter of rich pictorial quality, reveals a different character and temperament. He was first of all a still-life painter. The Budapest museum has a fine dynamic seascape by him in dark colours (Plate 47).

For lack of *vedute* we present Jan Beerstraaten's painting of a village and a funeral procession (Plate 48).

The material discussed here is only a small part of the Dutch landscape paintings in the Budapest Museum of Fine Arts. Several interesting paintings—some rare ones too—by the same masters and by others, are also treasured in our gallery.

LITERATURE

For detailed data and literature concerning the pictures published in our selection, see:

Pigler, A.: *Országos Szépművészeti Múzeum. A Régi Képtár Katalógusa* [Museum of Fine Arts. Catalogue of the Gallery of Old Masters]. Budapest, 1954.

For literature on Dutch landscape paintings in general:

Fromentin, E.: *Les Maîtres d'autrefois*. Paris, 1876.

Bode, W.: *Rembrandt und seine Zeitgenossen*. Leipzig, 1906.

Eisler, M.: *Rembrandt als Landschafter*. München, 1918.

Grosse, R.: *Die holländische Landschaftskunst*. Berlin, 1925.

Rosenberg, J.: *Jacob van Ruisdael*. Berlin, 1928.

Huizinga, J.: *Holländische Kultur des siebzehnten Jahrhunderts*. Jena, 1932.

Gerson, H.: *Philips Koninck*. Berlin, 1936.

Graf Raczynski, J. A.: *Die flämische Landschaft vor Rubens*. Frankfurt, 1937.

Stechow, W.: *Salomon van Ruysdael*. Berlin, 1938.

Knuttel, W.: *Hercules Seghers*. Amsterdam, 1941.

Stechow, W.: "Esaias van de Velde." *Nederlands Kunsthistorisch Jaarboek* 1 (1947) 83.

Friedländer, M. J.: *Essays über die Landschaftsmalerei und andere Bildgattungen*. Den Haag, 1947.

Clark, K.: *Landscape into Art*. London, 1949.

Bengtsson, Å.—Omberg, H.: "Structural Changes in Dutch 17th-Century Landscape, Still-Life, Genre and Architecture Painting." *Figura* 1 (1951) 13—56.

Bengtsson, Å.: "The Rise of Landscape Painting in Holland, 1610—1625." Stockholm, 1952 (*Figura* 3).

Van de Waal, H.: *Jan van Goyen*. Amsterdam, 1957.

LIST OF PLATES

PLATES

I

HENDRICK AVERCAMP
(1585–1664), worked in Amsterdam and Kampen

Winter Scene with Skaters

No. 1698. Oak, diameter 30.5 cm.
Signed on the left, on the wall of the house, with letters HAV written one into another.
Purchased from the art dealer Ferenc Kleinberger, Paris, 1899.

This animated little picture of white-silvery tones with pleasant and humorous genre scenes has a transparent glaring. The vivid local colours of the figures stand out against the general white effect. It is a characteristic and attractive creation of Dutch landscape painting of the early 17th century still rooted in Flemish mannerism.

DIRCK DALENS

(about 1600–1676), The Hague school

LANDSCAPE WITH BATHING SHEPHERDESSES

No. 248. Oak, 36.3 × 54.3 cm.
From the Esterházy Collection.

A fascinating creation, it proves a thorough study of Italian ideal, idyllic landscape painting early in the century. The master recalls Claude with his concept and is under the influence of Flemish masters too with his silvery-green colours. The tiny red harebells, small spots on the shore of a lake, make a vivid contrast to the light-green general effect, but are just enough to avoid monotony. The bathing nude turning her back on us recalls Italian reminiscences copied from an etching of his master, Moses van Uyttenbroeck. However true and subtle the master's observation of nature, still the scenery changes into an arcadic grove in which the shepherdesses give the impression of bathing nymphs. This painting has so far been attributed to Uyttenbroeck, substantial analogies however convince us to class it among the works of Dirck Dalens. A replica of the picture, also under the name of Dalens, was in 1932 included in the London collection of R. H. Ward.

3 DIRCK DALENS

LANDSCAPE WITH BATHING SHEPHERDESSES, detail

4

CORNELIS VAN POELENBURGH
(about 1586–1667), Utrecht school

CHILDREN OF FREDERICK V, ELECTOR OF THE PALATINATE AND KING OF BOHEMIA
(The eldest boy and girl in the role of Meleager and Atalanta)

No. 381. Oak, 37.9×65.5 cm.
Signed below, to the right "CP. 1628".
From the Esterházy Collection.

The painter put his colourfully dressed figures in a fresh green spring scenery of downs and painted a lovely hunting still life in the right foreground. We recognize Poelenburgh the landscape painter's style in the background. Before a bright blue sky some rose-coloured ruins are on top of a hill, a motif never missing from his pictures. The hilly background on the right side proves that the master was well acquainted with the Flemish masters and the Italian landscape painters of his time. A picture of a similar subject of the painter can be found in the Museum of Speyer and in the former Cremer Collection, Dortmund. Several copies were made of the painting (in the collection of Conte Barbiano di Beligioiso, Castello Sforzesco, Milan, and Hampton Court).

5

JAN ASSELYN
(1610—1652), Amsterdam school

ITALIAN LANDSCAPE. With the apse and *campanile* of the church of SS. Giovanni e Paolo in Rome

No. 239. Canvas, 67 × 80 cm.
From the Esterházy Collection.

The monumental block of the Early Christian basilica built of pink-coloured bricks rises against a sky with fleecy clouds on Monte Celio. The river on the right and the distant mountains are bathed in golden sunlight. Characteristic Italian figures are talking in the foreground. The artist painted the landscape from his memory, but he made on-the-spot sketches of the building. There is a similar picture of the master in the Schwerin Gallery. His drawing of the church of SS. Giovanni e Paolo is in the Albertina, Vienna.

6

PIETER VAN LAER

(1582—1642), worked 1623—1639 in Rome, otherwise mainly in Haarlem

Landscape with Morra-Players

No. 296. Oak, 33.3 × 47 cm.
From the Esterházy Collection.

A typical work of the artist painted in Italy. Behind the group of simple men playing, a scenery scorched in the wild Italian heat, a huge fortress-like building of small bricks before a sky of deep blue. A smaller replica is to be found in the Alte Pinakothek, Munich.

7

JAN BOTH

(1618—1652), Utrecht school

Antique Ruins on the Seashore

No. 390. Oak, 54.6 × 45.3 cm.
From the Esterházy Collection.

The golden mist of sunset is pouring over this southern seashore. In the foreground are the ruins of an antique building, at the foot of which Italian popular figures are chatting. The emptiness of the right foreground is filled out with the figure of a man riding a mule. Around the medieval buildings in the middle distance a busy group of tiny figures and wharfing boats; the clear air is in a golden hue by the rays of the sun setting beyond the distant mountains. Both's picture is one of the most Italianate pictures of Dutch landscape painting in the Budapest museum. The artist made several variations of this theme (Dresden, Richmond, etc.).

JAN BAPTIST WEENIX

(1621—1663), Utrecht—Amsterdam school

ANTIQUE RUINS

No. 232. Canvas, 80.5 × 68.3 cm.
Signed on the architrave: "Weenix Gio. Batt."
From the Esterházy Collection.

The right foreground is filled with the Tempio di Vespasiano, the ruin of a huge church in the Forum Romanum. The monumental tranquillity of this antique building, still half hidden in the earth at that time, symbolizing the past, stands in keen contrast to the fresh and vivid scene on the seashore in the background. As it was a custom with the Italianizers, the artist put next to one another different buildings and sceneries that do not belong together in reality. Behind the Temple of Vespasian he painted an imaginary obelisk, and a castle with bastions in the background, perhaps the Castello in Ostia. This is all the more probable as he painted a seaport with ships and many figures in a light of the sunset beside it.

9   JAN BAPTIST WEENIX

Antique Ruins, detail

REMBRANDT HARMENSZ. VAN RYN and GERARD DOU

Rembrandt (1606–1669) worked in Leyden and mainly in Amsterdam, Dou (1613–1675) in Leyden

Parable of the Man Hiding Treasure (Matth. 13: 44)

No. 342. Oak, 70.5×90 cm.

Made about 1630. According to several scholars, the figure and landscape were made by Rembrandt, the still life by Dou.

From the Esterházy Collection.

A work of the young Rembrandt, 24 years old at the time, created in the spirit of Seghers, especially as far as the landscape is concerned. Both the figure and the leaf of a great burdock boldly painted in the foreground suggest Rembrandt's brush. The background running into a great distance, the strange tower-like building and the trees beyond, which may be scarecrows of straw or haystacks or real trees, the mountains of fantastic shape closing the scene, the greyish-green tone and loose brushwork, are equally characteristic of Seghers' and of the young Rembrandt's landscapes.

REMBRANDT HARMENSZ. VAN RYN and GERARD DOU

PARABLE OF THE MAN HIDING TREASURE, detail

JAN VAN GOYEN

(1596–1656), worked in different places, mostly in The Hague

SEASCAPE WITH FISHERMEN

No. 4305. Oak, 36.1 × 32.2 cm.
Signed below on the left, on the boat: "VG"
Bequest of Count János Pálffy; from his Pozsony (Bratislava) palace.

This small painting is one of the masterpieces of the artist. It is also very characteristic of him with its low horizon, cloudy sky and monotonous bluish-grey tones. The picturesque sketchy figures of fishermen are working in the misty sea air.

13

JAN VAN GOYEN

VIEW OF DORDRECHT

No. 4205. Canvas, 83.7 × 128 cm.
Signed left below, on a pile standing out of the water: "JvG 1650".
Bequest of Count János Pálffy; from his Pozsony (Bratislava) palace.

Here the air is mistier than on the preceding painting. The view of Dordrecht from the island in the Oude-Maas was painted by numerous other painters. The usual diagonal composition leads the eye to the centre and to the left into a far distance: towards the farthest horizon where sky and water merge almost unnoticed. Similar landscapes of the artist are in the Rijksmuseum, Amsterdam, and in the Louvre.

JAN VAN GOYEN

VIEW OF DORDRECHT, detail

JAN VAN GOYEN

SEASCAPE WITH STORM

No. 4277. Oak, 37 × 56.8 cm.
Signed left, on the side of the landing boat: "JG".
Bequest of Count János Pálffy; from his Pozsony (Bratislava) palace.

Brownish-grey sea with waves lashed up by the storm. Boats are rolling on the rough but small waves. Sky and water are nearly the same colour, the sky lighting up only on the left side, its pink patches giving the sea a rosy hue.

WOUTER KNIJFF

(1607–1693), Haarlem school

BUILDING ON THE RIVERSIDE

No. 339. Oak, 39 × 55.6 cm.
From the Esterházy Collection.

This follower of van Goyen presents a typical motif of his master in this landscape. Though the motif itself may be similar to van Goyen's, its elaboration is much more schematic. The spontaneous ease of the great master becomes a manner. The technique is patchy, characterized by a certain clumsiness. The trawlers are standing stiff in the water, the stiffness is to be observed also on the figures. The misty sea air is not as palpable as with van Goyen, the distant sailboats and the windmill among the trees are patchy, however they do not give the impression of being seen through misty air.

SALOMON VAN RUYSDAEL
(1602–1670), Haarlem school

AFTER RAIN

No. 260. Oak, 56 × 86.5 cm.
Signed below to the right: "SvR 1631".
From the Esterházy Collection.

This early work of the master has much in common with similar early paintings of Jan van Goyen both for its motif and its yellowish tone. A house standing among a group of trees is to be seen beyond the sandy foreground, a coach crowded with passengers is approaching it. Left in the foreground hogs are wallowing, to the right among the cottages a solitary horseman is trotting. As in most of his early pictures, the scenery is closed by a cloudy sky like a backdrop.

SALOMON VAN RUYSDAEL

The Tavern

No. 294. Canvas, 91 × 136.5 cm.
Signed below to the right: "SV Ruysdael 1649".
From the Esterházy Collection.

This is a work of the artist's mature period. The scenery opens up in the background unto a distant horizon where the church of Beverwijk is visible. The contours of a tree leaning to one side and a covered waggon coach are outlined against the sky. A gay, loud and bustling company arrives to the tavern on the right, on the left a passenger is leaving the tavern in the coach. The tone of the picture is no longer yellowish, the foliage is vivid green, the sky is blue with bright white clouds.

SALOMON VAN RUYSDAEL

THE TAVERN, detail

SALOMON VAN RUYSDAEL

Tavern with a May Pole

No. 299. Canvas, 80.5 × 111 cm.
Signed below to the left: "SV Ruysdael 1664".
From the Esterházy Collection.

A late work of the artist even more complicated than the preceding one. The horizon with the river opens up diagonally in the background, buildings, however, are crowding in the centre and a diversity of figures, perfectly characterized by a few strokes of the brush, are swarming about them. A many-coloured puddle attracts our attention in the foreground with hogs in it, the water reflecting also a cow which is about to drink and the figures around it. The Groote Kerk of Alkmaar served as the model for the church.

SALOMON VAN RUYSDAEL

Tavern with a May Pole, detail

ANTHONY JANSZ. VAN DER CROOS

(1616/7—1662), The Hague school

LANDSCAPE WITH FISHERMEN

No. 251. Canvas, 86.5 × 110 cm.
Signed below, left: "AV. CROOS. F. 1651".
From the Esterházy Collection.

A strong influence of Jan van Goyen, as indicated by the yellow tones, the diagonal composition, the tree almost bare and the figures in a wide open scenery. The huge wicker fish-baskets in the left foreground give the picture a special charm. On the right the small town is reflected in the rippling water, large-sized figures and the baskets are outlined on the distant horizon in the foreground, in the background small sailboats and, beyond them, an even smaller windmill.

23

JACOB VAN RUISDAEL

(1628/29–1682), worked in Haarlem and Amsterdam

POND IN A FOREST

No. 263. Oak, 66 × 48.9 cm.
An early work of the artist.
From the Esterházy Collection.

We are taken to the depth of a forest, to a place where one gets very rarely. But this place is neither dark nor unfriendly, to the left in the background trees become thin, the rays of the sun break through the grey clouds and illuminate a bare tree-trunk. The silence of nature is disturbed only by the waterfowl frisking about in the pond. As a contrast we are reminded of mortality of life by the old tree-trunk almost deprived of its bark and by a watching owl on one of the branches. It is the work of a master with a romantic, melancholic and poetic fancy, who is a keen and devoted observer of the tiny elements of nature: grass, flowers, etc. This is a picture akin to the signed works of the artist from 1646-47 (Hamburg, Leipzig, Karlsruhe).

24

JACOB VAN RUISDAEL

DETAIL OF AMSTERDAM. Bank of the Binnenamstel, with the tower of the Zuider-kerk in the background

No. 4278. Canvas, 52.5 × 43.5 cm.
Signed below, right, on the plank: "VR".
Painted about 1660.
Bequest of Count János Pálffy; from his Pozsony (Bratislava) palace.

With this poetic and atmospheric representation the great master raises *veduta*-painting to the level of artistic landscape. A man wrapped in a black cloak is approaching the town on the yellow, sandy road. A pink-roofed cottage is standing on the riverbank. Some sailboats are landed before it with sails partly hoisted, partly hauled down and swayed by the wind. The contours of a town are outlined against the illuminated sky in the background. The vivid green tree proves the art of an excellent master of painting forests. The clouds in the sky seem to change their shape before our eyes.

JACOB VAN RUISDAEL

DETAIL OF AMSTERDAM, detail

MEINDERT HOBBEMA

(1638–1709) , Amsterdam school

Landscape with Cottage

No. 3321. Oak, 53×65 cm.

Signed below, left: "M. hobbema".

Purchased at the auction of the Vienna M. v. Königswarter Collection in Berlin, from E. Schulte, 1906.

An intimate landscape characteristic of the artist. He represents a scenery inhabited by man, with a cottage giving the impression of an illustration from a fairy-tale with its pointed roof. Before it a guelder-rose bush is flourishing, the family are chatting in front of the door. Trees are seen on the left, their foliage reflected in the water. Great white clouds of midsummer are sailing in the sky. An early work of the master, made about 1660.

27

JAN VERMEER II VAN HAARLEM

(1628-1691), Haarlem school

HAARLEM VIEWED FROM THE DUNES OF OVERVEEN

No. 4260. Canvas, 77.5 × 101 cm.
Bequest of Count János Pálffy; from his Pozsony (Bratislava) palace.

The monotony of the flat, wooded, sandy scenery is animated with a small Baroque house built of brick. The harmony of green, light-yellow and pink was a feature of his paragon, Jacob van Ruisdael, who painted the same motif himself. Only one or two church towers and a monumental block of the St Bavo Church are to be seen of Haarlem's blurred view in the background outlined against a distant light sky. The picture has so far been attributed to Jan van Kessel. Similar paintings of the artist depicting the same subject can be found in the Wallraf-Richartz Museum of Cologne, the Louvre (from 1675), and in the art trade.

28

CORNELIS GERRITSZ. DECKER

(d. 1678), Haarlem school

Inn "To the Goose"

No. 309. Canvas, 69 × 89 cm.
Signed right, on one board of the fence: "Decker f."
From the Esterházy Collection.

Nothing but an inn-sign on a strange four-gabled cottage among trees and flowers shows that it is a tavern. The well, made up of tree-trunks, increases the romantic atmosphere of the picture. The elaboration of the trees, the vegetation and the composition itself show the influence of Jacob van Ruisdael, though this picture is more crowded and fantastic than Ruisdael's romantic and poetic yet always airy representations.

29

DUTCH PAINTER, SECOND HALF OF THE 17TH CENTURY

Castle at Kostverloren

No. 258. Canvas, 64.5 × 79 cm.
From the Esterházy Collection.

This noteworthy picture is akin to the art of Jan van Kessel and Meindert Hobbema and represents the medieval castle at Kostverloren, near Amsterdam. The rendering of the details remind us of the former master, the elongated figures, however, of the latter. His preference for stronger colours is also indicative of Hobbema's influence. The motives recall the common ancestor: Jacob van Ruisdael.

30

ROELOF JANSZ. DE VRIES
(1631/2—1681), Haarlem school

The Highway

No. 273. Oak, 46×62 cm.
Signed below, right: "R vries".
From the Esterházy Collection.

Sand-colour and green, these two characteristic hues of Dutch sceneries prevail in this picture, where the artist proves to be a follower of Salomon van Ruysdael and of Jacob van Ruisdael. The great tree extending diagonally into the picture, divides it into two parts; the left part is crowded with houses, the right one would be rather dull and empty were the dissonance of the composition not compensated by the moving, luminous clouds. The two peasants talking to each other in the road are typical figures of the local Dutch landscape painting.

31

ROELOF JANSZ. DE VRIES

RIVERBANK

No. 267. Oak, 51 × 44.5 cm.
Signed under the dried-out tree, on the bank: "RVries".
From the Esterházy Collection.

Jacob van Ruisdael's favourite motif, a light tree-trunk, deprived of its rind, suddenly appearing in a green forest, is seen in this picture. It also shows the influence of Salomon van Ruysdael first of all in depicting animals. This picture takes us into the world of solitary mood of nature.

32

JAN DE LAGOOR

Worked in the middle of the 17th century, Haarlem school

WOODLAND

No. 261. Canvas, 77.2 × 68.7 cm.
Signed below, right: "JD. Lagoor".
From the Esterházy Collection.

The depth of the wood is painted in the spirit of Jacob van Ruisdael; the immobility and silence of the scenery is undisturbed. In the middle distance the tiny figures of the shepherdess sitting on a clearing and of the small animals are nearly lost under the huge trees. Such a classicizing relationship of figures and nature is frequent on French landscapes. The whole conception of this almost idyllic scenery proves the master's knowledge of classical landscape painting.

33

SIMON DE VLIEGER

(1601/2—1653), worked mainly in Delft and Amsterdam

LANDSCAPE WITH RIVER AND TREES

No. 323. Oak, 70 × 61 cm.
Signed below, left, on a dry twig: "S DE VLIEGER".
From the Esterházy Collection.

Though the number of figures in this picture are the same as in the former—only a hunter with his dogs chasing a hare—this painting of the many-sided master is an airy and dynamic work. As on his seascapes, here, too, he applies strong light effects. The wonderful, lonely scenery, far from any inhabited place, is full of life with its stooping trees, its clouds outlined against the sky, with the tree tops swaying in the wind and the pink lights shimmering through the foliage. Of the very few paintings of the artist showing wooded scenery the one in the Stockholm museum and also depicting hunters is most closely related to our picture.

34

JAN WYNANTS

(1630/35—1684), worked in Haarlem and Amsterdam

ROAD NEAR THE WOOD

No. 188. Canvas, 64.5 × 87.5 cm.
Signed below, right: "J Wynants 1667".
From the Esterházy Collection.

The master was especially interested in thistles and grasses, in creepers and sedges; there are hardly any pictures where he did not paint one or the other. In the foreground of this picture we can see a giant thistle with big leaves represented with an utmost minuteness and realism, next to it a lying, dead tree-trunk and behind them withering trees with almost no leaves on them: vegetation struggling on poor soil. Still, the scenery is silvery-green, humidity nourishes the sandy soil, and the rays of the sun are also as golden as after a good rain.

JAN WYNANTS

Road near the Wood, detail

ALLAERT VAN EVERDINGEN

(1621—1675), worked in Sweden, then in Haarlem and Amsterdam

The Skirts of the Village

No. 4291. Canvas, 76 × 66.5 cm.
Signed on the wall of the house to the left: "Av. Everdinger".
Bequest of Count János Pálffy; from his Pozsony (Bratislava) palace.

In his picture representing ramshackle cottages and courtyards with people, the artist recalls Scandinavian sceneries and buildings. A swift rivulet in the foreground and a small house built of pine-trunks, on the right, prove it. However, the Gothic church tower shooting up into the sky is rather characteristic of Dutch landscapes. It is a painting of exceptional freshness and quality made by a master who was extremely fruitful though often repeated himself.

37

AELBERT CUYP

(1620–1691), Dordrecht school

Cows in the Water

No. 408. Oak, 59 × 74 cm.
Signed below, left: "A. cuÿp".
From the Esterházy Collecton.

Though a fresh sea wind is chasing the heavy rainclouds, a golden light is shed over the flat piece of land, the gently rippling water, the motionless fishing boats in the background and over the cows in the foreground. Their mild tranquillity increases the immense calmness and silence of the picture. There is a similar picture by the artist in the Hermitage, Leningrad, and in the Robarts Collection, London.

38

AELBERT CUYP

Cows in the Water, detail

39 ANTHONIE VAN BORSSOM
(about 1629–1677), Amsterdam school

RIVERBANK WITH A SOLITARY HORSEMAN

No. 187. Canvas, 55.5 × 72 cm.
Signed below, right: "AVBorssom-f."
From the Esterházy Collection.

This fascinating scenery radiates peace and tranquillity. A solitary horseman in red clothes, sitting on a white horse, beholds the immobile nature: dunes crossed by canals, the endless plain and clouds heavy with rain. With the red clothing of the horseman, a colour similar to Cuyp's palette—though a tiny spot—the painter breaks the monotony of the greenish-yellow tone.

40

PAULUS POTTER

(1625–1654), worked in Delft, The Hague and Amsterdam

LANDSCAPE WITH A SHEPHERDESS AND A FLUTING SHEPHERD

No. 51.2885. Oak, 67 × 114.5 cm.
Signed below, left: "Paulus Potter: f."
From the Ráth György Museum in Budapest, 1951. Purchased from the Mauthner von Markhof Collection in Vienna.

It is an early and outstanding masterpiece of the painter. His way of looking at the landscape reveals the influence of the Dutch followers of Elsheimer, and of artists preceding Rembrandt. The brownish-yellow and silvery tones with tiny flowers in various colours shining out of the background testify to the influence of Pieter Potter, the father of the master. The lovely figures recall those of the mythology of classical landscapes. Akin to the master's signed paintings from 1642–44.

PAULUS POTTER

LANDSCAPE WITH A SHEPHERDESS AND A FLUTING SHEPHERD, detail

PHILIPS WOUWERMAN
(1619–1668), Haarlem school

ROCKY LANDSCAPE WITH TRAVELLERS AT REST

No. 51.789. Oak, 45.5 × 61 cm.
Signed below, right: "PHS W".
Purchased in 1951.

In the foreground, in the depth of a ravine, men and women and a horse, baggage on its back, prepare to leave. Behind it, to the left, there is a block of buildings upon a rock, obstructing the view toward the rising sun. Its rosy radiation is not only illuminating the sky on the left, it is also reflected on the tarpaulins of the covered waggons and on the shining body of the horse. The blue colour of the sky, the building of Italian character, as well as the figures themselves, give the whole scenery an Italian touch.

43

AERT VAN DER NEER

(1603/4—1677), Amsterdam school

Village Street

No. 198. Oak, 40.3 × 53.5 cm.
Signed below, right, with double initials: "AV DN".
From the Esterházy Collection.

The painting has a subtle brownish-green tone unvaried by local colours and a gloomy atmosphere. The way in which the master paints the tree-trunks from the wood on the left and in the background, standing parallel, and the diffusion of the mist and light among the trees are very characteristic of his brush. We see only a few figures in the broad street; the artist was attracted first of all by the atmosphere of the scenery after rain.

44

AERT VAN DER NEER

TOWN AT DUSK

No. 199. Oak, 37 × 53 cm.
Signed below, somewhat to the right from the centre, with double initials: "AV DN".
From the Esterházy Collection.

Widely opening landscape with light appearing in several spots. The rays of the setting sun make the clouds shining on the left side, but we can feel the night creeping into the town from the forest on the right. The artist was interested mostly in the reflection of flaring lights in the water.

45 SIMON DE VLIEGER
(for particulars see No. 33)

FREDERIK HENDRIK VISITING THE DUTCH FLEET ANCHORED AT DORDRECHT IN 1646

No. 314. Oak, 60 × 83 cm.
Signed on the boat to the left: "s DE VLIEGER".
From the Esterházy Collection.

Boats seem to cover the horizon in this lovely picture with its strong effects of light. The sunshine is glimmering from behind the thin clouds and the lights are strongly reflected in the still water. This typically Dutch scenery, wonderfully animated, attracts our attention with its freshness. The picture was made about 1650. The same subject is depicted in the artist's signed paintings in the Vienna Academy (1649) and in the Fitzwilliam Museum, Cambridge (1651).

46

WILLEM VAN DE VELDE, THE YOUNGER

(1633–1707), worked in the Netherlands and London

SEASCAPE

No. 216. Canvas, 50 × 66.5 cm.
Signed below, right: "Velde de Jonge 1653".
From the Esterházy Collection.

Anchored ships in a calm, immobile bay, veiled in a thin layer of mist, strongly illuminated. The artist proves to be a pupil of Simon de Vlieger as the ships drawn with infinite minuteness and devotion interest him much more than the slightly rippled, transparent water.

47

ABRAHAM VAN BEYEREN

(1620–1690), worked in The Hague, Leyden, Delft, Amsterdam and Alkmaar

ROUGH SEA

No. 252. Canvas, 69.8 × 112 cm.
Signed on the side of a sailboat in the foreground: "AVB f."
From the Esterházy Collection.

The small boats, as if made of paper, roll dangerously upon huge grey waves lapping before a dark, stormy sky; buildings, and a tower of a church, are in the background. What fascinates us most is the energetic brushwork of a painterly character, and that is why we regard Beyeren the landscape painter as a forerunner of Impressionism.

48

JAN BEERSTRAATEN

(1622–1666), Amsterdam school

THE VILLAGE OF NIEUKOOP IN WINTER WITH A CHILD'S FUNERAL PROCESSION

No. 53.496. Canvas, 91.5 × 128.8 cm.

Signed below, in the middle: "Nukoop naar leeven gedaen door J. Beerstraten".

Bequest of Count Jenő Zichy from the Vienna collection of Count Edmund Zichy.

With its dry technique, exact topography, fine, thin tree-trunks, elongated noble figures, this is a typical work of its master. The picture shows skaters in the foreground, a Gothic church to the left with a funeral procession, and a small village in a winter scenery in the background. The same village with the church and the funeral procession is shown in two more paintings of the artist (Kunsthalle, Hamburg, and Leeuwarden Museum).